TRAGEDY OF WHISPERS

Emmanuel Darasimi

Tragedy of Whispers

TRAGEDY OF WHISPERS

(A panthering refrain of frayed thoughts)

Emmanuel Darasimi

Emmanuel Darasimi

Copyright ©2016 **Emmanuel Darasimi**

ISBN: **978-978-958-500-7**

All rights reserved.
No part of this book may be reproduced, distributed, stored in a retrieval system, or transmitted, in any form or by any means, electronic, electrostatic, magnetic tape, mechanical, photocopying, recording, or otherwise without prior written permission from the Publisher.
For information about permission to reproduce selections from this book, write to info@wrr.ng

National Library of Nigeria Cataloguing-in-Publication Data

Cover Design: Grafix Pluz

Printed and Published in Nigeria by:

Words Rhymes & Rhythm Limited
Suite C309, Global Plaza Plot 366, Obafemi Awolowo Way, Jabi District, Abuja, Nigeria.
08169027757, 08060109295

www.wrr.ng

Contents

DEDICATION 8

ACKNOWLEDGMENT..9

OCEANS OF LUST 12

A GROOVE OF NUKES 13

AN EXPENSE ON GREED 14

MICHAEL GEEKS 15

BLISS OF FOUL 16

GRIMINESS OF SORROW 17

SHOTS OF JOY 18

THE BEAUTY OF LUST 19

THE HEARSAY OF REALITY 20

DREAMS ARE TREASURES 21

MERCHANTS OF FRIGHT 23

SONS OF THE PSALM 24

A BALLAD OF POLITICAL PARASITES 25

DREAMS OF ELROY 26

EMPERORS OF CRIMINI 27

SOCKS OF INTEGRITY 28

LIONS DETHRONED 29

SAILS OF REDEMPTION 30

FAREWELL	31
OLOLUFE	33
JEALOUS	34
IFELEWA	35
BALES OF BLISS	36
A SULTRY FLAIR	37
TALES OF ORENTE	38
BEAUTY MADE CROWN – [A.A]	39
I MISSED YOU TODAY [O.I]	41
THIS LITTLE HEART	42
THE WAY I FEEL	43
A QUEEN'S HEART – [G.T]	44
MY 'PYT'	45
IYA DARA	46
MOCKERY OF MANTLES	48
EVIL GRACE	49
SOJOURN OF THE PROPHETS	50
CAUSATION OF TIME	51
GOD'S SIN	52
KINDRED OF HOPES	53
GUARDIANS OF MERCY	54

SABBATICAL SEAMS 55

CHARMING HELL 56

A CURSE TO SERVICE 57

HUMILITY 59

ODE TO SUCCESS 60

SOMEWHERE IN THE SAVANNAH 61

AFFILIATIONS OF KNOWLEDGE 62

MELLOWS OF MONDAY 63

PASSIONATE PRINTS 64

A NIGHT WITH PEARLS 65

A TEMPEST OF SARCASM 66

A NOTION ON EMPHASIS 67

WHY NOW? 68

FLAWLESS by Adeyemi Temi 70

Author's Contact Details 71

Emmanuel Darasimi

DEDICATION

*For you, the dreamers
Overlooked at school
Never won prizes*

You own tomorrow

ACKNOWLEDGMENT

I thank God. In the process of putting this book together, I realized how true this gift of writing is for me. You have given me the power to believe in my passion and pursue my dreams. I could never have pulled this off without your strength and grace.
To my parents, Bola and Bola Fajounbo, I am utterly speechless! I can barely find the words to express all the love, wisdom and support you have given me and how well it has impacted me. Though this publication would come as a surprise, I hope you love it. My siblings, Temi, Dolu, Pelunmi, Dunmininu, thanks for being the very best.
I would love to appreciate profoundly the Vice Chancellor, University of Ibadan, Prof. Abel Olayinka and his beautiful wife Dr. Wunmi Olayinka for their unending support towards the realization of this passion. In that vein, I am hugely indebted to Emeritus Prof. Ayo Banjo, Prof. Hyginus Ekwuazi, Prof. CBN Ogbogbo, Dr. Yinka Egbokhare, Dr. Charles Akinsete, Dr. Adams Akewula and other staff whose words of encouragement and unending support academically and motivationally have influenced this publication. It's been an honour associating with you by virtue of this book. I have learnt a whole lot from you.
Next up, I would love to thank the *Tragedy of Whispers Team* for performing exceptionally well and giving their very best into this dream. To my media team headed by Ayo Adeagbo – CEO, XtremeMedia; my ever talented graphics designer, Paul Boniface – CEO. Grafixpluz Designs; my team of editors headed by Adenekan Adedapo & Kolade Freedom and the WRR Management, for their pressure, creativity, patience,

corrections and most importantly commitment. Special thanks to Sanya Solomon, Adebayo Olabanji and Ipadeola Bernice for being there to support the project inspite of the challenges.

A big shout out to Adeoye, Gbemisola, Temitope, Olayeni, Damola and all friends and colleagues who inspired it but would not read it!

Tragedy of Whispers promises to be only the beginning.

Tragedy of Whispers

*Let us embrace the trust
Of life's ceaseless battles
For our brightest hopes
Ignite from the darkest place*

OCEANS OF LUST

Indebted by unheard whispers
I looked but looped not
Pondering hard on fascistic salvation
Tended to desires with wools of deceit
I conquered but wasn't crowned

Our uncanny love for selfishness
Deterred visions of glorious prosperity
We robed our shame in greed
Trudged our dreams in wheels of death
As oceans flooded our hope

We need only excel
In ways of goodness
Spiced with graced mercy
Despising not ages of anguish
But acknowledging hopes of healthier years

Our oceans flourish only when founded
On rhymes of sobriety and propriety

A GROOVE OF NUKES

Their rivulets of pain
Led to plains of anguish
Seconds transmuting to eternities
…of agonies descending to prick our hearts
Another throne disengaged

Like a stab on our souls
It kept ticking, asserting violence
In hearts athirst of chaos
To rejuvenate the fears of many
Dis-affording the living another chance

To reassert our stance
Against animals suited as human
All we need do is prosper to win
A sacrifice to retain victory
Then prosper again.

Emmanuel Darasimi

AN EXPENSE ON GREED

A million views ago:
...was the distance of lack from reality
We auctioned crumps of dreams
And sold fleets of vision

We loved vanity rooted
In moral decay and absurdity
Purchasing only lust
An amount unwilling to beautify
With fees of priority

Maybe…if my soul tarried
With flashes of luxury
I could price joy
And its succor would feel my anguish
Staked deep down.

MICHAEL GEEKS

Michael!
Come break me,
Bake but don't taste,
Caution with no ammunition,
That gait of yours;
Pondering the streets
With witty wonders
Stealing affections with dabs
In an array of tender hearts
Praying love becomes endless…

Emmanuel Darasimi

BLISS OF FOUL

A culture oiled by richness
In a civilization of deceit –
Attestation to longevity

Like green bales
The blend manifests
In shadows of morality

Denim in quest with the skies
Turns deaf to uniqueness
Like snows trying to un-whiten

And when the sons
Of these juvenile clans
Try to set the ashes
Of unflattering history ablaze
Let culture merry.

GRIMINESS OF SORRROW

Blessed in still feelings
My absurdity amazes self
In tailing my sorrows
The future frowns…

Sieged with insecurity
Drained in stale emotions
You tale my miseries
Rerouting whirls of success

My epic fears
In attesting to these visible evils
Cries to conquer
Tomorrow's dream

Partnering with empathy
The griminess lingers...
In tracts of hard work and bravery
Founded on dried tears
You tale my success still

SHOTS OF JOY

A feat laudable
After ardent commitment
And placement of all hands
On a dusty deck…

Answering cajoles
Of unfamiliar resentments
And memories of creativity
Align our needs with celebration

As we raise our glasses
In conformity to these joys.

THE BEAUTY OF LUST

The hotline of weed aired
While the bling track echoed
In merriment of loss
Grooving with our frenzy airmax

I silently texted the city
Watching the pages of funk
As the beauty of love emerged
From the shame of the smoky screen
A soldier's heart is silenced

Displaying the love for coco in HD
Beauty avoided the gaze of guilt
Following the ladder of conviction
My grievance hammering on trust
Still within the confines of conformity

With feelings of defiled nostrils
We voicelessly voiced in volumes
Of un-displaying lust
As we ponder on what purpose and hope are left
When we aren't chanced to define wrong...

Emmanuel Darasimi

THE HEARSAY OF REALITY

I desire a trust
Unscarred and rejuvenating
In the abyss of my soul
When the grease of morality
Shackles my whispers

I beseech a voice
Cranky and luscious
In tides of hypocrisy
When fountains of lust
Hinder my panther

I solemnly pace
In strides of hope
And unnerved history
Let change merry.

DREAMS ARE TREASURES

Every dream lays a path
Membered by disbelief
Curdled in discouragement
Saturated in frays
Of unending hopes

Every dream brooks an ocean
Seared in goodwill
Wavy on passions
And unmerited dexterity
Of graced inspirations

Let's bud our dreams
In bits of purpose
Unperturbed by frayed reality
And sky-fall of promises
We own tomorrow.

Emmanuel Darasimi

*Never before
Had I wanted to say so much,
But said so little
Felt so much;
But stayed so silent*

MERCHANTS OF FRIGHT

To whom shall I turn?
When royal oaths remain belittled
Scarred in jaggedness of feudalism
… An upturn of self-patronage

To whom shall I turn?
No sorrows or miseries too deep
To warriors that owe self selves
Enlivening null, inspiring void

To whom shall I turn?
When the gates of bravo open forth
Like a jawless mouth reaching for a prey
Bringing through spirits of chariots past

To these shall we turn:
Knights of unremorseful courage
Relinquishing the machinery of warfare
In a web of undeniable heroism
And a stance of communal inspiration

Emmanuel Darasimi

SONS OF THE PSALM

We attired elegantly for the ball
Fitted to our countenance of shame
Our beautiful robes of deceits
Shone brightly amid merriments
Of outstanding failures and losses
We sons of the psalm!

The courtier opened our hearts
With undaunted performances of ruse
Praises, peppered by aggressive swag,
Proclaimed the king's naivety
The crowd roused, cheered on
We sons of the psalm!

Halting the show of prideful idiocy,
One of the king's many princesses
Along with the hubby, the heir
To the throne of political annihilates,
Bowed as they stepped into the gallery
We sons of the psalm!

Enchanted by the predatory crowd
Psalmists played disgruntled harps
Sharpening tones of hatred
To vibes of un-bankrupted vices
Pleading with reasons in rhymes
We sons of the psalm!

A BALLAD OF POLITICAL PARASITES

A solider of solitude
Afraid of attention
Beams of bravery
Reflect its rarity
Basking in breakthroughs

We are a compendium
Of selfish brushes, taxing
on democratic hunger
Money, the will for its roundness

For a generation of political loafers
A wishful redemption it is
For a class who values less
Unperturbed of the gavel of integrity

And if our stands are firm
In an atmosphere of wastage
I seek a worthy desire
To Salute!

DREAMS OF ELROY

In a flash of worries
Deserving of graceful awards
Inspiring accomplishments
In gathering of lacks
Success realizes reality

In making an unjust right
I seek airless answers
To the end of hunger
Pondering on stomached deficit
I wept.

EMPERORS OF CRIMINI

'A billion recovered
No bills footed'

As the smoke shadows your bandits
The fire devours
In celebration of fraud
We foretell the chaos adequately

'A bandit captured
Your bondage cloaked by truth'

Anticipating your downfall
Advocated by men of honest reports
A time of reckoning stares us
Its nearness moist our faces

'A boulevard of justice
Infested by brats of double standards'

Emmanuel Darasimi

SOCKS OF INTEGRITY

We got king-size impunity
And testimonies of lie
In alliance with our greediness
We stammered in discontent

We achieved coloured reflections
Into the toes of reality
Allowing us a wander in our conscience
To keep our deceit for warmness of change

We remembered morals;
Our fetes of integrity
Seating and gazing in anticipation
To protect, palliate and comfort.

LIONS DETHRONED

In hallows of rumors
We beautified tragedy
With ornaments of trust

In loneliness of change
Our councils' prettied revolutions
Consumed by depths of pain

The drill went on
For a decade of rotten hopes
A lifetime of anonymity for justice

Emmanuel Darasimi

SAILS OF REDEMPTION

Let me tussle with the tides
Flameless in waves
Of butchered remembrance

Facilitate my un-stomached infrastructure
On roads of Ingvar promises
In journals of historical propaganda
Entrenched with empathic campaigns

And when the shores of redemption align
Saturate my every march
With grains of unrevoked revolutions

FAREWELL

To a morality of hopes
Petrifying and unrelenting
farewell...

To a savagery of promises
Blindly echoing in bars
Of dispirited vibes
farewell...

To a loop of trust
Defiled and betrayed
In corridors of power
farewell...

To the soul of belief
Weak and tired
farewell...

Emmanuel Darasimi

*I would fill the pages of every book
With words that trace the curves of your skin
And will never be done with you*

OLOLUFE

Your gait parts the eyes to enchant the heart
Your smile heals with a mantle of dimples
Your gaze brings the stars to my *mind step*,
It eclipses the sun at day, the moon at night.

Let's take tonight with us
In tribute of your dauntless meekness –
Gum to the sole of my feet on your floor
Ololufe, none can gauge your beauty…

On this path of unending affection
We shall fold ourselves on grasses
Made green by waters sourced
In the dam of your dewy heart

Dawn paws upon us
With the cosmos of emotions
No exit for our limbless love

JEALOUS

The rain rambled
Beaming a tragedy of lust
On your glamorous skin
Marked with countless fingers
of unknown palms…

Your shadow drowns me
In solitude of your flame
The night's loneliness pierces my soul
Reminding me only of your absence
Endless it would seem…

The love remains unquestioning
Though the splashes spike lavishly
And the night nauseates my soul
I remain loyal to the rains…

IFELEWA

Her beauty, a conquer of wars
Her smile, a cure for sorrow
Her eyes, a diviner for fidelity

The beauty of your love
Emboldened by your meekness
Gives eyes to my yearnings

Your hairs un-amounted
The number of years I'd love you
Recklessly and unremorseful

Emmanuel Darasimi

BALES OF BLISS

In a field scented by serenity
And a moment of saturation
I ran across the field of beauty
Fulfilling the lust of my lungs
And the restlessness of my fingers
I skimmed in appreciation

In jealousy of your uniqueness
In rows of exciting vegetation
I re-affirmed the bliss
Of such heavenly branch
As I lay on the beds of bales
Beauty's beauty is indeed reassured.

A SULTRY FLAIR

As her mosaic butt rippled
And her jugs resurrected
In the abyss of my mind
I remained mutter-less

As she strode in near coalition
Of her Elroy legs
In the walkway of my fantasies
My zipper grumbled

And then she did sit
Amongst deterring fantasists
Their one vivid imagination
Crossing her thighs conspicuously.

Emmanuel Darasimi

TALES OF ORENTE

My imaginations – a record re-beaten
My thoughts – un-channeled
Gloriously feasting on her blemishes
Tasking my heart to her flame

A luck of smiles assimilated
Petrifying my every thought
Her cheeks – an assembly of dimples
Reaching for a galaxy of compliment.

BEAUTY MADE CROWN – [A.A]

In this quest for unloveliness
A rendition of beauty
Taxed by my frantic zeal
To let go
Demystifies my resolve
As I pen down passion-imbued prints

Ever since you cared modestly
Regret sprung on every page
And I owed you all my flaws
Crucifying my every mistake
From that gay night

Your sensual dint on my lips
On that road of untarred mastery
Betrayed the depth of my esophagus
While we tested the matrimony of our hearts
In those split seconds of bliss
She refused any touch

Silence and then unbelief
At the width of my vocal trap
In rending her joy
She did let the smile on
The chuckles came in contentment
Of a rumored truth

Now….In frustration of the truth
Trouble brewed in our carelessness
Causing sparks of untapped tempers
We did fall:

Emmanuel Darasimi

An amazing splinter of friendship
A jealous sadness it sprouts

Evidently still,
In ranges of communication
Sabotaged by new language
And twinkles of endless art
My prints of passion would remember you

I MISSED YOU TODAY [O.I]

Like a shadowy mist
You remain unhindered
In the corridors of my mind

For a million crowns,
Rearming through my heart
The quest is yet voyaged

I realize the tragedy
  Of not letting go
    As I whimper in fading inks…

Emmanuel Darasimi

THIS LITTLE HEART

Admissible to the senses
By desires that reign
Through the devotion of my heart
To an elusive mystery

The truth mirrors disdainfully
As it remains anonymously vain
Through the lens of my lover
Who is often insane…
To the tragedies of my heart

With my every enquiry
I seek a blissful fairy
Championed with an income
To broadcast my love supreme
In an endless whisper of promises

THE WAY I FEEL

She came dignified
Like something beyond freshness
But I wasn't impressed

I needed her mental dexterity
I needed her mentally dressed
I wanted a glimpse at her soul
Not in blemishes of her best

Emmanuel Darasimi

A QUEEN'S HEART – [G.T]

I never knew hearts
Could hit notes like this
A tempo of parlayed love

I always knew they could sing
But never imagined the beat
Hitting the cords of agape

When the thought to give up flashed
You held my hands confidently
And suddenly everything felt alright

Your deeds have charmed their way
Into realms of fulfillment
Conquering thrones of beauty

I could hear your smile
When you heard my voice
Saying in apt confidence;

*"I would sift every woven thought
in your lovely mind just to ensure my palace
stands in the abyss of your heart"*

MY 'PYT'

In pearls of emancipated smiles
Unrelenting in its savagery
I remember your chuckling simplicity
Bold and contagious.

I desire beauty
Franchised in lusty dreams
And toppings of cuteness
Sane and true.

Hurt remains void
In jades of endless promise
A willfully creaked cheer it is...
 Rich and understanding.

IYA DARA

Iya Dara...
A virtuous woman purer than dew
With a body as alluring as the ocean's
On tides of the rivers of flawlessness
Down into the waves of beauty
Mantles her ever glowing grace

She inspires righteousness
In passages of uprightness
Her lights can't be shut out by shades
As she wheels the patent of sunrays
Harnessed in unconditional love

Iya Dara...
A kettle of inspiration
Whistling for an eternity
A tone of encouragement and confidence
In an outpour of endless commitment
On burners and flares of near confusion

As the sun rises once more
I am reminded that you're the reason
It finds me waiting and smiling
In appreciation of your sacrifice
A constant reminder of my mortality

Tragedy of Whispers

*Forever you remain
A symbol of indelibility
In exalted monuments
Standing on unfaded glory
Ageless*

MOCKERY OF MANTLES

It gathered as clouds
Inhabiting our seers' skies
With pulpits resting in electronic birds
Winged by deception – a wasteful flight!

Prophets without pastoral grace…
Pray for my penniless soul
As I walk these vast lands with aching soles
For surely, your deliverance costs!

Akpos says it's a ministry of prosperity
Even when your mirrors don't reflect me
They needn't expand this horizon of satires
For nothing cracks our ribs more than your anointing
Indeed! I portray ingenuity.

While they perform on altars of tiled dollars
I seek refuge only in the truth
Because when the day sets
Our faithful walks shall outlive your ruse.

Tragedy of Whispers

EVIL GRACE

Unfounded and uninhibited
You showered me with love for hatred
In resentment of godliness

Saturating my heart,
With deeds of shameless passion
I merry gallantly

Whimpering in majestic disdain
My flesh propelled me on
Disbanding realities of salvation

Grace as indeed arrived
Bringing tidings of judgement as guests
An affliction on my thoughts

And as the cup of anointing rolls forth
I forfeit its clamor and glamour
Embracing the gamble of favor casually

Uncertainty reigns supreme
As I witlessly conjure memories of
My fellowship with the supreme deity.

SOJOURN OF THE PROPHETS

In beat-less abandon
A spark of empathy
Beseeched our morality
Putrefying the need to reflect

Guiding against recurring temptations
It bleared our emotional resolve
As we never did forget the cost
Unconquered by our alpha parents

Drowning the voice of reason
In rounds of ammoniated sins
Sermons become rebels
Against our passion for freewill

We are quick to forget history
Even in realms of whispered visions
The prophets remain prophetic
Relinquishing celestial memories.

CAUSATION OF TIME

The matters keep a glow
Like a dip in time
In a mystic of seconds
In articles of depiction
It is a tire

On altars of revolutions
Its words, a diary of dollars
Belittling the passion of my jaws
A sad truth.

GOD'S SIN

His efforts were shamed
In a misery of visions
Contemplated in centuries of ruins
Belittled by lusty worship

Ridiculed into power
A chance to be free
A world to conquer
As mere fallings reign

The supreme mourns
In disappointments and regrets
In this generation of retrials
Nothing crummy to grade the deity
Except the ineptness of sins…

KINDRED OF HOPES

Like an abandoned faith riddled with tautologies
It lingered in our Jerusalem of thoughts
Giving us a priceless audience
To foresee a better forever

In our exchange for a storm less sea
Our boat crews 'of superficial fears
Tire the tides of our heart with uncertainty
…we anticipate a faceless titanium

Butchered for the quest
Cursed in the name of salvation
Bathed with charms of resentments
We found the beam

As the stars journey
We follow suit like the wise three
Good being our only passport
Selflessness, an eternal passenger

And with merciful hearts
The kindred make worthy hosts
Of a generation of truth –
A chance to finally treasure hope.

Emmanuel Darasimi

GUARDIANS OF MERCY

Your pricelessness eagers me
In search of an opportunity
To be *messiahied* by budding portions
Then shall I celebrate

For I hunger and lust for mercy
My tears have become a dead sea
My paths deviate dry lands
In a countdown of passion

Look into my heart
Only then would you realize
How the thirst encompasses all
Cropping none out

My pleas kneel before your confidence
To borrow that portion
Till barons know the value
And brooks overflow in passion

…find it in your grace
When your patrol draws near
To associate with my presence
And dine in the remains of my sacrifice.

SABBATICAL SEAMS

The message echoed
In homes of empty ambitions
Where hearts are re-broken

The creator, a patent
Of patience in testaments old
Reflect on lived times

Waiting on fairness
Even as he lost his sabbatical
To the lust of the naira

We await the reawakening
When hallelujah shall be anthem
On days of our breaths.

Emmanuel Darasimi

CHARMING HELL

We forsake the love
That bows to us
And folds our wants
In attention yearned

In seconds of lust
We skydive momentarily
To a hellish field
In a trust of burns
By malicious charm...

A CURSE TO SERVICE

Coated in oversized blazers
Tied in conspicuous neck pieces
Their feet paced brogues of repetition
Armed with over memorized beatitudes
Doctored by hours of biblical rage

Beautiful it would seem
When words become an alteration
Of belittled prophecies
Consummating grains of history
Their fate triumphs over faith

Unconditional it would seem
When sweats of service
Soaks distressed oil
Flowing in salvation
And agony of the cross

Emmanuel Darasimi

*I envy the brains
That are sure of the path
Who let their dreams lie brightly
In textbooks of unhindered creativity*

HUMILITY

…mildly illuminating our love
From iconic spheres of deeds
It splintered conversely;
Our love for identical ingenuity
Broadcasting needs of the ancestry
As our passion plies pardon

When strife becomes championed
To call creativity on the line of honesty
We beseech royalties of diplomacy –
Progenies of Einstein
Earners of the pen
With no disdain or heartache

Emmanuel Darasimi

ODE TO SUCCESS

The game chasers are feeble-footed
Screams of rest hold them bound
Momentary rewards blind their mind
To infinite revelations o success

Reflecting deeply on ashen endeavors
Knowledge is severely solicited
As it toils on sandiness of opportunity
And glorious peaks of accomplishments

Hasn't it been declared?
We are to grab greatness by its horns
In this endless race of *out wittiness*
Battered by hard work and discipline
And undefined successes

SOMEWHERE IN THE SAVANNAH

We ducked as the wind
Slapped our amused faces
The tour was fascinating
With heels of discoveries
Reeling at our unfamiliar feats
Entangled in our wills of vision

Never contemplating new hopes
We kept whispering our discontent
While we thirst for intellectualism
...gagged, throat-bound.

The sands of sanity promised our joys fame
But all routes to dynamism barricaded
We were reminded of today's tomorrow
...somewhere in the savannah.

Emmanuel Darasimi

AFFILIATIONS OF KNOWLEDGE

You enthroned
A betrayal of wit
To the hastiness of my soul

Misery, an overseer
To the sorrows of my heart
As tears become fueled
By my report's easel of shame

Curtailed by pain
Grade points sustained the bane
Remaining unaffiliated still
As the flow of GPs deceived

The lust of degrees
Perches on misconception
Distilling colourss of brilliance
In a wager for classism

All I ask amidst turmoil
An understanding of creativity
All I seek among answers;
The fruits of knowledge.

MELLOWS OF MONDAY

It called out loud
As the sun pierced through the blinds
Brimming the room with grim effort
Sketching greatness on walls of labor
Rekindling the will to succeed
Luxuries of the extinct week, forgotten

I answered!

Emmanuel Darasimi

PASSIONATE PRINTS

We let our hearts flourish
In amazement of creativity,
Unearth my discouragements
While we pen our passions
In lines of unending devotion
To inspire ceaseless memories

The prints revolve with commitment
In a cestrum of progress
And apt faith in change
Championing the zeal for fortitude
We let our lamps shine so bright
A light that blinds the groom

What more can we ask?
Like the rise of the phoenix
We cultivate flames in our dreams
As every need becomes tales
On inks of passionate prints.

A NIGHT WITH PEARLS

In a twist of fragile braids
Their eyes twitch in a moon of torches
Defying the night's call for cosines
Amidst frowns of tiredness
The insects feast, in solidarity

As the night sipped their zeal
The pages flipped, consolidating boredom
Insomnia for knowledge
Strutting on creeks of brilliance
Yawns become an epilogue of their eyelids

They drowned revisions in ink
The speechlessness in their aura
Molded with hunger for distinct grades
Burned the cold in their courage
Censoring not the hustle

for
A
1st
Class
Flight

Emmanuel Darasimi

A TEMPEST OF SARCASM

Reciting a fuss of flares
We troubled a purpose-minted cause
Dullness on our shapeless *tom fords*

Our generations' splintered inventions
Crucifying roarings of endless silicones
Allowing greed a collective past

And as we promise a rejuvenated freedom
The Krebs key collectively into creativity
Illuminating our visions.

A NOTION ON EMPHASIS

I want to think
In cradles of knowledge
Valued on my passion

I want to grow
With hormonal hard work
Titling on mantles of integrity

I want to prosper
In heights of cosmos
Grooving on satisfaction

I want to inspire
Flooding oceans of hope
For a cause to beautify a fruitful mind

Emmanuel Darasimi

WHY NOW?

It came knocking hard
On our resolve to flex
In seasons of fun

It pounded violently
On an eternity of turn ups
In clubs of soft work

And like a cold supper
The frowns of laziness
Spread its content

Vandalizing untapped inks
On sheets of memorized guess
As our over dabbed brains slept

THE ART OF BRILLIANCE

In paces of uncultured nerds
Glowing in savaged attention
I wrestled with grades

Inking notes in summaries
On sheets of crumbled guesses
And unlicensed answers

In arrays of knowledge
Brilliance remains *DIS-arted*
Beautifying colonies of tsunami

In this path of imagination
The plains are clearer now
Subtle but indeed reassuring

FLAWLESS by Adeyemi Temi

I tend to varnish in your sight
In compliments of the world, brightened
Your face – a predator; chasing darkness into cradles
I feel lost in the complexity of your paradise heart
I'm thirsty and quite hasty for your ebony self

Your beauty is like the sun,
That tends to set not
For your prime ushers
The rebirth of a jasmine empire
Filled with the glee of unchanging temperance

Tragedy of Whispers

Author's Contact Details

Email: knightdarseus@gmail.com

WhatsApp: +2349031330139

Instagram: knight_darseus

Twitter: Emmanuel Darasimi

www.ingramcontent.com/pod-product-compliance
Lightning Source LLC
Chambersburg PA
CBHW051349040426
42453CB00007B/493